An Introduction to

English Glassware to 1900

I

Interior view of Apsley Pellatt's
Falcon Glass-house, Southwark,
from his *Curiosities of
Glassmaking* (1849)

An Introduction to

English Glassware to 1900

Charles Truman

Assistant Keeper, Department of Ceramics
Victoria and Albert Museum

LONDON: HER MAJESTY'S STATIONERY OFFICE

Series Editor Julian Berry
Designed by HMSO/Graphic Design
Printed in the UK for HMSO

ISBN 0 11 290411 4
Dd 718115 C 65

HER MAJESTY'S STATIONERY OFFICE

Government Bookshops

49 High Holborn, London WC1V 6HB
13a Castle Street, Edinburgh EH2 3AR
Brazennose Street, Manchester M60 8AS
Southey House, Wine Street, Bristol BS1 2BQ
258 Broad Street, Birmingham B1 2HE
80 Chichester Street, Belfast BT1 4JY

*Government Publications are also available
through booksellers*

The full range of Museum publications is displayed and sold at
The Victoria & Albert Museum, South Kensington, London SW7 2RL

Since glass is so commonplace in modern life we scarcely give a second thought to its manufacture. It might therefore be advantageous to outline briefly the techniques involved in its production before tracing the development of glass in England.

At its purest, glass is silica, fused at a very high temperature, but in order to reduce that temperature alkali fluxes may be added. The glass-maker can find silica in a number of natural forms, the most usual being sand, flint, quartz, or certain pebbles, and the fluxes used might be soda, obtained from burnt sea plants, or potash, from burnt bracken or beechwood. Lime, which also assists in the fusing of glass, normally occurs in sand and was not usually added to the 'batch', as the mixture of constituents is known, by English glass-makers. Since the fused mixture is often slightly coloured with a greenish or brownish tinge, a decolourising agent, such as manganese, 'glass-maker's soap', could be added. The material from which glass is made is called 'metal' by a glass-maker. This is to avoid the substance, glass, being confused with the utensil, a glass.

The first indications of man's discovery of glass occur over three and a half thousand years ago in Mesopotamia (modern Iraq). Early vessels were formed by trailing molten glass around a core which was subsequently removed but some time during the century before the birth of Christ, Middle-Eastern craftsmen discovered the technique of blowing glass.

Glass-houses were usually small businesses which moved wherever custom or the availability of fuel led them. To heat the furnace to melt the batch, large quantities of fuel, at first wood but later coal, were necessary; and the supply of fuel, together with a supply of fireproof clay to contain the molten glass at high temperatures, were the overriding concerns for siting a glass-house.

With the Roman invasion of Britain in the first century AD the art of glass-making was brought to this island. Roman glass-workers used a soda-lime glass obtaining their alkali from burnt sea plants, a recipe which was to be used for about the next thousand years. Excavations of Roman sites in Britain have revealed several glass-houses, the most notable being at Wilderspool in Cheshire, Caistor in Norfolk and Colchester in Essex. With the collapse of the Empire,

Roman influence, owing its designs largely to glass produced on the Syro-Phoenician coast, diminished and plainer wares began to predominate. Many of these so-called Teutonic glasses from the fifth to seventh centuries have survived since the pagan customs of Britain's new invaders led them to bury glass, amongst other wares, with their dead. Cone-shaped beakers, some with finely trailed decoration, or beakers with 'claws' of glass applied to their sides are amongst the grandest pieces; but lesser goods, palm cups, jars and bottles have survived and may well have been made in England, probably in Kent, at least as early as the seventh century. We have evidence that glass-makers were summoned to Monkwearmouth from Gaul by Benedict Biscop in 675 and from Mainz by Cuthbert in 758, and excavations have indicated that both vessel glass and window glass were made there. At Glastonbury, a glasshouse was operating in the ninth and tenth centuries, and other sites have revealed enough fragments to show that there was a considerable amount of glass-making in England at that period.

About AD 1000 glass-makers turned from the traditional Roman recipe for glass and began producing glass fluxed with potash obtained from burnt beechwood or bracken. Because of the source of its constituents this glass is frequently referred to by its German name *waldglas* (forest glass) or less often by its French name *verre de fougère* (bracken glass). This change coincides more or less with publication of the technical manual *Diversarium Artium Schedula* by the German monk Theophilus. Book two of his treatise is devoted to the manufacture of glass, and describes tools, furnaces, and ingredients, as well as the production of window glass by the 'broad' glass method. This involves blowing a cylinder of glass which is then opened along its length and allowed to flatten while cooling. Such a method was adopted in Lorraine, whilst in Normandy in the fourteenth century the 'crown' technique of blowing a sphere, opening it and spinning it flat, was developed.

During the Middle Ages, glass-making in England appears to have been concentrated on the Weald of Surrey and Sussex, and what evidence there is of production relates mainly to window glass. In 1276 mention is made of one Laurence Vitrearius (the glass-maker), of Dyers Cross near Chiddingfold, who supplied the glass for the east windows of Westminster Abbey, and in the following century John Alemayne, presumably a German, of Chiddingfold who made the glass for the windows of St. George's Chapel, Windsor, and St. Stephen's, Westminster. In 1367, Alemayne leased property to John Schurtere, 'glasier', and at least three generations of Schurteres were involved in glass-making in the Weald.

A variety of vessels survive in fragmentary forms from the period 1000 until the mid-sixteenth century, but they number so few that it is unwise to try to distinguish an English style from that of the rest of north-west Europe.

Four main forms should be mentioned briefly here. First is the long-necked bottle known in Theophilus as an *ampulla*. Secondly funnel-shaped lamps, with broad but shallow bowls and conical stems hung from wood or metal chandeliers that are frequently depicted in manuscript illustrations. Thirdly from the thirteenth century, glass urinals began to appear in profusion. These broad-rimmed bag-shaped vessels were used both as chamber pots and for the medieval medical practice of uroscopy. However, the grandest glass to survive from the fourteenth century is a group of drinking goblets with vertically ribbed bowls set on perilously thin stems which rise from domed bases. By the beginning of the fifteenth century these elegant glasses gave way to beakers, some ribbed, others with glass added about the foot, and others plain. Since we know that glass was imported from Venice as early as 1399, it has been suggested that these vessels were directly influenced by Italian prototypes. However, it may be that the form comes from further east, from Byzantium, and arrived in northern Europe by-passing Venice altogether. All the wares produced in England were of common green glass (*waldglas* or *verre de fougère*). It was not until 1567, when Jean Carré arrived in London from Antwerp, that the production of clear glass to rival the Venetian *cristallo* began.

Carré was a Calvinist, born in Arras, who came to England because of the atmosphere of religious tolerance which prevailed under the reign of Elizabeth I. By July 1567, he claimed to have built three furnaces, two in Sussex at Fernfold Wood, and a third for the production of Venetian-style glass in London. Later the same year he was granted letters patent, with his partner Anthony Becku, for the production of window glass at his Sussex furnaces, which were run by two Lorraine glass-makers, Thomas and Balthazar de Hennezell, and two Normans, Peter and John Bungar. By October 1568 John Carré had begun the making of glass in the *façon de Venise* at Crutched Friars in London. The following year the de Hennezels left the business following a dispute with Anthony Becku about the training of English craftsmen. Carré clearly had a preference for foreign craftsmen and imported Venetian glass blowers to work in London. The first recorded is Quiobyn Tittery who arrived in 1570, and in 1571 probably the most famous of the immigrant craftsmen, Jacomo Verzelini, came to England from Antwerp. However, Carré died in 1572, and the company failed. But by 1574, Verzelini had acquired the Crutched Friars glass-house and in December that year he received a monopoly to manufacture 'drynkinge glasses such as be accustomablie made in the towne of Morano [Venice]' and to teach Englishmen 'the arte feate and mystery' of glass-making in the Venetian style [plate 3]. The letters patent also forbade its manufacture elsewhere in England and the importation of fine glass for twenty-five years.

The attribution of glasses to Verzelini's glass-house depends largely upon their decoration. Ten glasses are at present known to survive, each having a date upon it ranging from 1577 until 1590.

Nine of these glasses are engraved with a diamond point, the tenth, and latest, is gilt. Like the making of *cristallo*, diamond engraving was an alien art, first mentioned in English documents in 1589. During the period of Verzelini's monopoly, the name of only one engraver of glass has survived, that of Anthony de Lysle, a French immigrant working in the liberty of St Martin le Grand about 1585. It is therefore not unreasonable to assume that he was the engraver of the Verzelini group.

Verzelini acquired land in Kent to provide the wood to fuel his furnaces, and himself resided at the manor of Downe, whither he retired in 1592. His death on 20 November 1606 is commemorated by a monumental brass in the parish church.

The monopoly which Verzelini obtained was for making *cristallo* whilst other glass houses produced coloured or window glass. For example, the Venetian Sebastien Orlanden and the Frenchman Godfrey Delahay made 'bugles, amells and glas in collers' (beads, enamels and glass in colours) at Beckley in Sussex, and Alfold continued as a centre for the production of green glass into the seventeenth century. In the Midlands at Bishop's Wood, Eccleshall, the Henseys, Titterys and Tysacks were making window glass.

A new patent to produce *cristallo* was acquired in February 1592 by Sir Jerome Bowes, a former ambassador to Russia, and a member of the Court circle. Bowes, being unskilled in the art of glass-making himself, employed most of Verzelini's old craftsmen at a furnace built at Blackfriars and managed by William Robson and William Turner [plate 4].

Robson, who assumed sole control in December 1605, must be seen as the first native English maker of fine glass, and a constant adversary to the importers of foreign wares. By 1610 he had expanded his business by acquiring the glass-house at Winchester House Southwark, established in 1608 by Edward Salter, where *cristallo* was also made. However, in 1612, another patent for making 'all manner of glasses' was issued to Sir Edward Zouche. The significance of this patent, and the reason why it was claimed that it did not infringe others already in existence, was that it employed coal to fuel the furnace rather than wood. Since the first quarter of the sixteenth century, the English countryside had been gradually stripped of its woodland, not only for glass-making, which used huge quantities to maintain the furnaces at a high temperature, but also in the making of iron, and from 1610 development of the coal-fired furnace gained impetus in England.

William Robson ceased production in 1614 and in the following year a number of influential courtiers, amongst whom was Sir Robert Mansell, joined Zouche's prosperous company. Mansell soon acquired sole control of the company which had two furnaces, one at Winchester House, Southwark, and the other at Lambeth; he built another in Broad Street and put it under the management of William Robson. In 1620 the Venetian ambassador to the Court of

St James reported that glass made by Mansell rivalled that produced in Murano. Only fragments of glasses dateable to the period of Mansell's monopoly, 1615-42, have survived, but a list prepared in 1635 demonstrates the types of glasses that he made and sold. Three qualities of glass are mentioned: 'ordinary drinking-glasses', 'crystal . . . glasses formerly made and imported from Venice' and 'crystal . . . glasses—made by me (which never were before in this Kingdome) and of all fashioned that are desired and bespoken. Both beer-glasses and wine-glasses were made from these three differing types of glass or metal.

From the fragments which have been excavated, it is clear that in the early years of the seventeenth century, three stem forms were usual on wine-glasses: a tall inverted baluster; the mould-blown lion mask stem and the serpent stem said by Mansell to be 'of extra-ordinary fashions'. The beer-glasses, too, show three forms. The first is a slightly flaring beaker, often with a wrythen or a dimpled surface. The second form is a short beaker with flared sides, and the third is of cylindrical form decorated with a trailed spiral of glass and blown into a ribbed mould, with the foot embellished with a rigaree (wavy) trail of glass.

The outbreak of the Civil War saw the demise of the system of monopolies, and with the Restoration of Charles II a new and powerful body emerged. This was the Glass Sellers Company, who obtained their second Charter from the King in 1665, and acted as an intermediary between the makers of glass and their public. The business of two members of the Company, John Greene and Michael Measy, with their Venetian supplier Allessio Morelli is well documented by a series of letters dated between December 1667 and November 1672 preserved in the British Library. Accompanying the letters are drawings of the shapes favoured by English clients. Three bowl forms prevail: round-funnel, conical and flat-based conical, set on short stems with plain or ribbed knops. The smaller glasses are described as for wine, the larger for beer. The sheer volume of the orders from Venice is astonishing; over seven thousand glasses in a single batch, and there is every reason to suppose that Greene and Measey were not alone in the importation of glass to Britain.

Meanwhile in England the Duke of Buckingham established a crystal glass-house at Greenwich, and imported Italian craftsmen to man it in 1660. In the following year Martin Clifford and Thomas Plowden applied for a further licence to make crystal glass but they both entered Buckingham's service in 1662. The next year the Duke was granted the privilege of making mirror glass, and in 1663 he took over Thomas Tilson's patent for making plate glass, thus acquiring almost total control of glass-making in the metropolis. Not himself interested in the everyday management of the glass-houses, Buckingham employed John Bellingham from 1671 to run his concern for him.

Of considerable use to the English glass industry was the

publication in 1662 by Dr Christopher Merret of *The Art of Glass*, a translation of Antonio Neri's *L'Arte Vetraria*, which had been first published in Florence in 1612. It was Merret's stated aim to 'give some light and advantage to our countrymen of that profession', and his book may be seen as the culmination of Verzelini's promise to instruct Englishmen in the making of glass.

At this period one of the characters [plate 5] central to English glass history emerges. George Ravenscroft was for some years involved with the Venetian trade. His brother was in partnership with the English consul in Venice and, according to the Venetian ambassador in London, George Ravenscroft had amassed 'considerable capital' whilst in that city. In 1674 he was supporting in London two Italian craftsmen as well as importing Venetian mirror glass into England.

Ravenscroft had established a glass-house in the Savoy, London, in July 1673, and in the following year he approached the Glass Sellers Company with samples of his 'particular sort of Christalline Glass'. He had petitioned the King for a patent to make this glass a month earlier in March 1673/4. The Glass Sellers were clearly delighted with Ravenscroft's efforts and supplied him with premises at Henley-on-Thames where he could continue his experiments and make glasses to their design. His crystal glass contained a proportion of lead oxide (lytharge) in the batch. Such an inclusion was not new. Indeed it is recommended by Neri for the making of paste jewels, but his recipe was not suitable for the production of vessel glass. Ravenscroft's contribution was to have produced a lead glass with all the refractive qualities sought from paste jewels combined with the ductility of *cristallo*.

However, initial production was frustrated by a tendency of the glass to *crizzle*, that is to be rendered slightly opaque by the presence of a multitude of internal fissures [plate 6]. By late 1676 or early the following year Ravenscroft was able to advertise a new metal, identified on the glass by a seal bearing a raven's head, which was not subject to crizzling. It should be pointed out, however, that much glass bearing this seal is crizzled today but the process of decay is a slow one and it must be supposed that the new metal remained clear long enough for Ravenscroft and the Glass Sellers to dispose of the pieces marked in this way. Several glass vessels which bear the raven's head seal mark have survived: bowls, some with stands, roemers [plate 7] (from the German for Roman, and denoting, at this period, a round bowl supported on a thick stem with applied prunts, that is to say blobs of glass), serving bottles, beer mugs, jugs, posset-pots and stems of wine-glasses. The principal forms of decoration, which are given in Ravenscroft's own price list of 1677, are vertical ribbing and 'nipt diamond waies' (a diaper pattern formed by converging ribs).

By 1678/9 Ravenscroft had ceased to supply the Glass Sellers Company but the company very probably obtained lead glass from other makers in London. Two other firms are known to have produced lead glass at this period, Michael Racket in the Minories and John Bowles and William Lillington in Stony Street, Southwark, who may have marked their glass with a seal mark bearing the letter S, as found on two intact glasses, which stylistically appear to be contemporary with Ravenscroft. It is clear that the secret of lead glass was quickly disseminated, and by the early 1680s several glass-houses advertised the production of 'flint glass', a name synonymous with lead or 'crystaline' glass. Hawley Bishopp took over Ravenscroft's Savoy glass-house in 1681/2. Another glass-house in the Savoy was run by Henry Holden but it is apparent that no lead crystal was made there until the concern was taken over in 1689 by Phillip Dallow. In Salisbury Court, off Fleet Street, a glass-house was reopened in 1684 to make flint glass and the Duke of York's furnaces at Redmead's Lane, Wapping, were certainly producing lead glass at the same time. In 1693 Francis Jackson and John Straw advertised lead glass being made at the Falcon Glass-house, and the partners owned another glass-house near St Mary Overies Church and a third in King's Lynn. In the last years of the seventeenth century lead glass was being made at sixty-one glass-houses including four in the Bristol area, five around Stourbridge, and at the Dagnia's glass-house in Newcastle-upon-Tyne. The Dagnia family held the monopoly of glass-making in Newcastle until 1728, when Joseph Airey and Isaac Cookson began production of flint glass.

It was during the closing years of the 17th century that a truly English style of glass evolved. Confident in the use of the lead metal, glass-makers produced bold forms developed from those which had been ordered by John Greene, whose simple forms and absence of ornament were paralleled in some contemporary silver. Although some trace of the Venetian style of glass-making was still evident, the influence of Germany, bolstered by the arrival in 1714 of a Hanoverian monarch, is felt more strongly. The German style may be seen not only in the glasses themselves (the roemer) and in the high-shouldered tapering stem (Silesian stem) [plate 11], but in the introduction of wheel-cutting to this country. This technique, which added a new dimension to the decoration of English glass, was adopted from the lapidaries and involved the glass vessel being held against an abrasive rotating wheel.

The year 1745 is seen by some as a watershed in the history of English glass for in that year a tax 'upon all the Materials or Metal or other preparations whatsoever that shall hereafter be made use of in making of all Crown Plate and Flint glass' was introduced to help finance an expensive European war. This Excise Act, claimed W. A. Thorpe (see Further Reading below), 'hampered English glass-making for exactly a century and ended by destroying the art of glass in England'. Naturally there was an outcry against this levy on the weight of the raw materials used in glass-making, and more so when it was doubled in 1777, but its effect on the style of glass should not be overemphasised. The lighter, ornamented glass which prevailed during the middle of the eighteenth century had roots in the period before the Excise Act. The Dagnia family in Newcastle, for example, had developed the so-called 'light baluster' before 1730. This lightness, both in weight and style, is surely paralleled by a similar feeling in other media during the manifestation of the Rococo style in England.

Several styles of stem dominate English glass in the mid-eighteenth century. The air-twist stem, formed by making air bubbles in a 'gather' (the molten matèrial picked from the pot) of glass and then stretching and twisting it into a stem, probably derived from glass-makers in the Low Countries, was introduced into England in the early 18th century [plate 15]. It had certainly gained popularity by the 1730s but its appeal was relatively short-lived and air-twists dating from after 1760 should be considered exceptional. The technique of wheel-cutting is found applied to the stems of glasses, and indeed to many other pieces, from the early years of the eighteenth century. English lead glass of the late seventeenth century is known to have been cut on the wheel, but it is rare to find facet-cut stems before about 1720. The fondness for cut glass developed throughout the mid-eighteenth century; the play of light which it caused in the metal being particularly sympathetic to the rococo mood [plate 23]. Stems containing twists of opaque white or coloured enamels seem not to have been introduced until the mid-1740s, the earliest dated example being 1747. Again their appeal seems brief and few can be dated after the 1760s. The technique of manufacture of these enamel twists was not new, since it is in many respects similar to techniques used by Roman glass-makers and later by Venetians and those working in the Venetian style.

As if by extension to the use of enamels in the stems of drinking glasses, the manufacture of glasses of coloured metal became popular in the mid-eighteenth century, generating a taste which lasted until the late eighteenth century, before being revived in the nineteenth century. It has been fashionable in the past to consider that certain colours were produced in certain areas, but this would seem to be an over-simplified view. Blue glass, for example, traditionally ascribed to Bristol, appears to have been made in London, the Midlands and Newcastle, whilst opaque white glass, which had been made in England at least since the seventeenth century, was certainly made in Bristol as well as the Midlands. Perhaps the exception is ruby glass, for which a German named Meyer Oppenheim of Birmingham, took out a patent in 1755 but who moved to France by 1780 following his bankruptcy in 1777.

An alternative method of embellishing a glass is by painting it with enamels, themselves glasses coloured by the addition of metals or metallic oxides [plate 18]. Despite the use in England of painted enamels on metal in the seventeenth century and their frequent use on glass abroad, enamelling on glass in this country is not documented until 1756. In the previous year William Beilby was apprenticed to an enameller in Birmingham. Beilby, together with his brother Ralph and sister Mary, adapted the techniques that he had learnt to enamelling on glass, probably after 1760 [plate 19]. Certainly by 1762, another decorator of glasses, Michael Edkins, was at work in Bristol. Since one of Edkins's ledgers survives, it is possible not only to determine his type of business, but to establish the names of the leading Bristol glass-houses for whom he worked. These may be mentioned here: Crittle and Longman of Redcliffe Backs, Longman and Vigor of the same address, William Dunbar of Bristol and Chepstow, Vigor and Stevens of Thomas Street, and Lazarus Jacobs of Temple Street. Several pieces of blue glass decorated with gilding bear the name of the latter's successor, Isaac, and it is not unreasonable to assume that this was the type of decoration added by Edkins between 1785 and 1787 when Lazarus Jacobs's name appears in the ledger.

Other workshops, such as that of James Giles in London, specialised in gilt decoration. Giles, who also painted and gilded porcelain, worked in Berwick Street and Cockspur Street, London from 1749 until his bankruptcy in 1776 [plate 20].

Following the Declaration of Independence by the citizens of North America in 1776, the excise on glass was doubled to generate sufficient funds to fight the rebels. Shortly afterwards, in 1780, Ireland was granted the right of free trade, giving an obvious incentive to English glass-makers to start manufacturing lead crystal, free from any restrictions of the tax on weight, in that island. Glass-houses in Dublin, Belfast, Cork and Waterford were largely staffed by immigrants from both England and the Continent, and it is in consequence difficult, if not impossible, to distinguish English from Irish glass in the absence of any firm provenance or mark. Furthermore, the tendency to ascribe the taste for heavier glass and deeper cutting to the freedom from tax of the Irish makers may also be misleading. Other branches of the decorative arts, particularly silver, show a marked solidifying of forms about 1800 and it could be argued that the change in weight of glass was as much dictated by fashion as by financial concerns.

The early years of the nineteenth century see an increase in the variety of vessels made in glass. Of these the jug, apparently rarely included in the glass-maker's repertoire since the late seventeenth century, is the most obvious, but other items, such as bowls, salts and dishes in glass become more common. And from the last years of the eighteenth century onwards, a new drinking glass form emerges. Although called a 'roemer', this glass differs from its antecedents of the same name since it has a conical bowl supported on a short stem. All these pieces display the ability of the English glass-cutters and this skill was emulated in France, Belgium and the United States of America. Patterns of cut glass in the early nineteenth century are characterised by mitre cutting, that is, V-shaped grooves, arranged in an horizontal canon, but by the 1820s pillar fluting, with the ornament arranged vertically, also becomes common.

One of the most decorative of techniques applied to glass at this period was the use of ceramic inclusions, called either 'sulphides' or 'crystallo-ceramie'. Originally developed in France, this technique was introduced into England in 1819 by Apsley Pellatt, of the firm of Pellatt and Green in London [plate 29]. This technique, which is described in Pellatt's *Curiosities of Glassmaking* (London, 1845), was both time-consuming and unprofitable and it seems that the firm did not produce 'sulphides' for long but the practice was revived in the late nineteenth century by John Ford of Edinburgh.

Although much cut glass was exhibited at the Great Exhibition of 1851, indeed the centrepiece of the whole exhibition was a cut-glass fountain over twenty feet high by F. & C. Osler of Birmingham, tastes were changing and by 1853, John Ruskin was not alone in the opinion that 'all cut glass is barbarous'. The taste for wheel-engraved glass, technically approximating cutting, continued however. For this, mostly immigrant Central-European craftsmen were employed, as wheel-engraving was an art practised in their native countries since the seventeenth century. By 1873, the Bohemian Paul Oppitz was working for W. T. Copeland, and Frederick Kny and William Fritsche joined the staff of Thomas Webb in Stourbridge shortly afterwards. Glass engraved on the wheel [plate 33], and polished in imitation of rock-crystal, became a speciality of the Stourbridge glass-houses. Under the direction of James O'Fallan, Kny and Fritsche worked this style, whilst at Stevens and Williams Joseph Keller and Frank Scheibner were engaged in similar work. A result of this skill in intaglio cutting was the development of cameo-cutting from the 1860s [plate 34]. The great protagonist of this art was John Northwood, whose vase engraved in relief with figures from the frieze of the Parthenon was completed in 1873. In 1876 he completed a copy of the Portland Vase, the first-century Roman cameo-cut vase in the British Museum. The Woodall brothers, Thomas and George, also worked on cameo-cut glass for Thomas Webb.

Akin to cutting in that it involved the removal of glass was the technique of etching. Certainly practised in the late eighteenth century, the true potential of acid etching was only developed in the 1830s. Thomas Hawkes of Dudley appears to have been the first glass-maker to realise the commercial possibilities of the technique, in which the glass was covered in a resist, usually of wax, and a design cut through to reveal the glass. This was subsequently immersed in hydrofluoric acid, which attacked the glass but not the resist, leaving a pattern where the resist had been removed. Indeed it is probable that Hawkes used the technique on the plates which he supplied to the City of London in 1837 for use at the first reception at Guildhall in honour of the new Queen Victoria [plate 35].

However, the gilding, printing and painting which give the plates such a grand effect obscure the precise method of their decoration.

A form of decoration which had the aspect of engraving or, more precisely, of acid etching, was patented in 1806 by John Davenport. This involved the application of finely ground glass which was subsequently fired on to the vessel in the same way as enamel. Glasses decorated in this way are often marked 'Patent' [plate 36].

Unlike the rest of Europe, England was slow to appreciate the possibilities of coloured glass. Bottle glass with splashes of colour was made by various factories in the early nineteenth century, notably at the Wrockwardine (Donnington) Wood glass-house in Shropshire, although not apparently at Nailsea, which glass-house has given its name to the type. However, by the 1830s many of the Midlands glass-houses were producing more sophisticated coloured glass, and in the 1840s the firms of W. H., B. and J. Richardson of Stourbridge and George Bacchus, Rice Harris, and Lloyd and Summerfirth of Birmingham exhibited cased (that is glass with a coloured outer surface) and cut glass. A further development was in the use of cased and cut glass over a silver finish. The process, which was patented in 1849 by Frederick Hale Thomson and Edward Varnish, consisted of depositing a layer of silver on the inside of a double-walled vessel and then sealing the two layers by means of a glass plug to prevent the atmosphere from tarnishing the silver. Since Varnish was a retailer it is probable that his glass was made by James Powell of Whitefriars. The use of enamels on glass was revived in the 1840s. Henry Cole (first director of the South Kensington Museum) in his alias Felix Summerley commissioned enamel-painted glasses designed by Richard Redgrave from the firm of J. F. Christy of Lambeth in 1847, and several pieces of glass in antique forms with enamel painting were exhibited at the 1851 Exhibition.

In the same exhibition several firms exhibited glass which derived its inspiration from Venetian glass of the Renaissance. 'Ice-glass' with a crackled surface, and glasses with enamel twist stems were shown for example by the firm of George Bacchus. This 'Venetian' influence may also have inspired the so-called 'fancy glass' of the later nineteenth century, which depended both on colour and trailed and pincered decoration for ornament. In this style the Stourbridge firms of Hodgetts, Richardson & Son, Stevens and Williams, and Webb excelled and produced all manner of novelties including vases, baskets, epergnes and flower stands. From the 1870s many new colours were developed, some whose constituents changed colour when heated, such as the Queen's Burmese Ware, introduced from America by Thomas Webb in 1886.

The technique of press moulding glass evolved in the United States in the 1820s and was adopted by European glass-houses soon afterwards. Apsley Pellatt toyed with the idea, and took out a patent in 1831 for moulding hot glass, but not actually pressing it in a reusable mould. The scent bottle in plate 40 shows the results of his experiments. The bust of William IV and the surrounding acanthus border have been moulded whilst the rest of the bottle has been cut on the wheel. However, it is evident that by 1837 the process had been perfected since press-moulded plates exist commemorating the accession of Queen Victoria in that year. The moulds for pressing glass were probably cut by die-sinkers in Birmingham and it is in the Midlands that the technique was first used successfully. Early pressed pieces either imitate cut glass, or have 'lacy' ornament overall to conceal the lines left by the joins in the mould. The process was adopted by many glass-houses throughout England but especially in Birmingham, Manchester, Warrington, Newcastle, Gateshead and Sunderland.

A revulsion against pressed and 'fancy' glass is seen in the glass made for the heralds of the Arts and Crafts movement. The architect Philip Webb designed for William Morris glasses of simple form excluding any ornament. These were made by James Powell and Sons and marketed through the firm of Morris, Marshall, Faulkner and Co. An even more obvious aversion to the slick products of most glass-houses is demonstrated by the 'Clutha' (Gaelic for the Clyde) glass made by James Couper and Son of Glasgow to the designs of Christopher Dresser and, later, of George Walton. This deliberately crude glass was quickly imitated by Powells, who named their product 'Old Roman'. Powells also produced a range of opalescent glasses in the Venetian taste, and their designers sought inspiration from glass depicted in paintings by Old Masters, some of which they copied directly. Thus we see how fine glass-making in England had come full circle, from Carré's Venetian glass in the sixteenth century to Powells in the late nineteenth and early twentieth centuries.

But despite the revulsion to cut glass amongst aesthetic theorists of the late nineteenth century, it was the English lead metal skilfully cut by English craftsmen that was the envy of Europe and this country's central contribution to glass-making internationally.

2
Claw beaker, probably sixth
century
Greenish glass, with applied and
blown out 'claws' and trailed
decoration
Found at Ashford, Kent
Transferred from the British
Museum
Ht 9⅜ in (23.8 cm)
C.187-1939

2

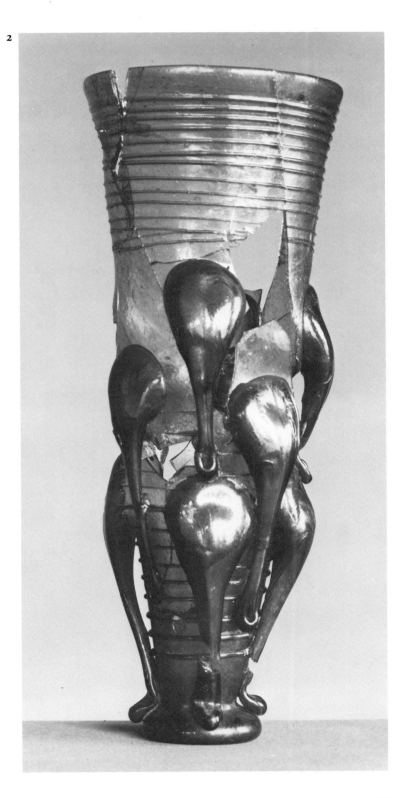

3
Goblet, dated 1581
By Jacomo Verzelini at the
Crutched Friars glass-house in
London
Glass engraved with a diamond
by Antony de Lysle
This goblet, one of ten which
survive from the period of
Verzelini's monopoly, 1574-92,
was made in 1581 for John and
Jone Dier.
Buckley Collection
Ht 8½ in (21.5 cm)
C.523-1936

4
Wine-glass, dated 1602
Probably by William Robson and
William Turner at Blackfriars,
London

Glass engraved with a diamond
The date, 1602, on this glass
suggests that it was made at the
Blackfriars glasshouse of Sir
Jerome Bowes who was granted
a monopoly for making
Venetian-style glass in 1592.
Rees-Price Collection
Ht 8 3/16 in (20.8 cm)
C.575-1925

5
The Butler Buggin Bowl, about
1676
Probably made in the Savoy
glass-house of George Ravens-
croft
Lead glass, engraved with a
diamond
The arms engraved on the bowl
are those of Buggin of North
Cray, Kent, and Burnett of Leys,
Co. Aberdeen, for Butler Buggin
who married Winifred Burnett on
16 July 1676.
A companion bowl is in the
Corning Museum of Glass, New
York
Ht 3 7/8 in (9.8 cm) Diam. 5 in
(12.7 cm)
C.143-1963

6
Ewer, about 1676
Probably made in the Savoy
glass-house of George
Ravenscroft
Crizzled lead glass
That the glass of this ewer is
crizzled, and that it does not bear
the seal mark used by
Ravenscroft from late 1676 or
early 1677, when he claimed to
have solved the problem of
crizzling, date the piece to about
1676.
Buckley Collection
Ht 10 3/4 in (27.4 cm)
C.528-1936

5

6

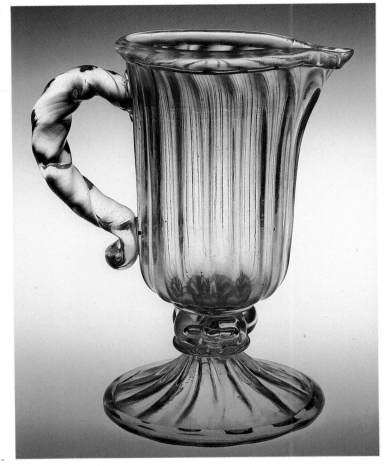

7
Roemer, about 1676-7
Made in the Savoy glass-house of
George Ravenscroft
Lead glass, mould blown, with
applied prunts (ornament applied
to the body of a glass vessel)
This roemer bears the raven's
head seal which was used by
George Ravenscroft from late
1676 or early 1677.
Buckley Collection
Ht 6½ in (16.5 cm)
C.530-1936

8
Serving jug, about 1680-85
Lead glass with mould blown
decoration
Although of lead glass, it is not
possible to attribute this piece to
any of the several glass-houses
who produced lead or 'flint' glass
in the late seventeenth century
Rees-Price Collection
Ht 7 in (17.8 cm)
C.580-1925

9
Goblet and cover, about 1695
Lead glass, with hollow stem and
finial, and with a folded foot
Massive goblets such as this
emerge in the late seventeenth
century and it is supposed that
they were used for drinking
toasts. The form, although
essentially English, is not too
dissimilar to that of the glasses
ordered from Venice by English
glass sellers.
Buckley Collection
Ht 14 in (35.6 cm)
C.536 & A—1936

10
Goblet, early eighteenth century
Engraved by George Chapman in
1761
Lead glass with diamond
engraving
Although the goblet dates from
the early part of the eighteenth
century, the engraving was added
by Chapman some years later.
The precise identification of the
symbolism of the engraving has
not been possible. Chapman is
known to have supported the
Protestant King William III but
the Red Indian fighting an
alligator may allude to the
capture of Quebec in 1759.
Ht 10⅞ in (27.6 cm)
C.127-1977

11
Wine-glass, about 1715-20
Lead glass, with a conical bowl
and 'Silesian' stem
Rees Price Collection
Ht 5⅞ in (14.9 cm)
C.156-1925

12
Wine-glass, about 1715
Lead glass, with a conical bowl
and 'Silesian' stem moulded with
the inscription GOD SAVE KING
GEORGE
Rees Price Collection
Ht 6⅜ in (16.2 cms)
C.135-1925

13
Wine-glass, mid-eighteenth
century
Lead glass, with a bucket-shaped
bowl and enamel twist stem
Rees Price Collection
Ht 5¾ in (14.6 cm)
C.324-1925

14
Wine-glass, mid-eighteenth
century
Lead glass, with a trumpet-shaped
bowl and straight stem enclosing
a 'tear-drop'
Rees Price Collection
Ht 6¾ in (17.2 cm)
C.462-1925

15
Wine-glass, mid-eighteenth
century
Lead glass, with a trumpet-
shaped bowl and air twist stem
Rees Price Collection
Ht 6¼ in (15.9 cm)
C.481-1925

12

14

13

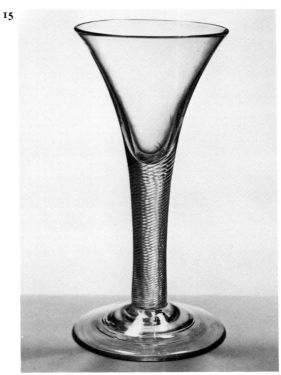

15

16

16

Bowl, dated 1764
Painted by an artist signing PP or PF
Opaque white lead glass, painted
in enamels
English glassmakers used opaque
white glass from the early
seventeenth century. In this case
the opacifier is arsenic but tin
oxide was also used. The birds
are taken from engravings by
Francis Barlow.
Mellor Bequest
Ht 3½ in (8.9 cm)
C.100-1947

17

Decanter and stopper, late 18th
century
Blue glass with gilt decoration
Decanters with gilt 'labels' were
decorated by Michael Edkins in
Bristol but it is not possible to
attribute this piece to his
workshop. The label indicates

17

18

that the decanter was intended to
contain Dutch gin
Buckley Collection
Ht 10⅜ in (26.3 cm)
C.750-1936

18
Decanter, about 1762
Probably made in Newcastle-
upon-Tyne and enamelled by
William Beilby in 1762
Lead glass, with painted enamel
decoration
The arms on the front of the
decanter are those of Newcastle-
upon-Tyne, and on the reverse of
Blackett of Co. Northumberland
Probably for Sir Edward Blackett
who became M.P. for
Northumberland in 1768.
Buckley Collection
Ht 9¼ in (23.5 cm)
C.620-1936

19
Wine-glass, about 1765
Probably made in Newcastle-
upon-Tyne, and enamelled by
William Beilby
Lead glass painted in enamel
This glass, which is of a type
known as a 'light baluster' , is
signed 'Beilby pinxit'. The coat
of arms is spurious but the
cartouche which contains it is a
good example of the Rococo
style.
Buckley Collection
Ht 7¼ in (18.4 cm)
C.623-1936

20
Bowl and cover, about 1770
Decorated in the London
workshops of James Giles
Lead glass, cut on the wheel and
gilt
James Giles was a decorator of
porcelain and glass with
workshops in Berwick Street and
Cockspur Street from 1749 until
his bankruptcy in 1776
J. C. Robinson Collection
Ht 6⅜ in (16.2 cm)
C.85 & a—1879

19

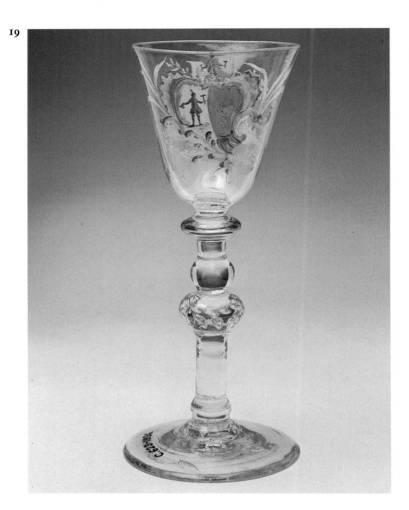

20

21

Wine- and cordial-glasses, about 1770.
Decorated in the London workshops of James Giles
Lead glass, cut on the wheel and gilt
The Neo-Classical decoration of these two glasses is characteristic of Giles' later work (see also plate 20). The facet cut stems and ovoid bowls are typical of English glass of the 1770s.
Ht of wine glass $4\frac{7}{8}$ in (12.4 cm)
C.151-1918
Ht of cordial glass $3\frac{3}{4}$ in (9.6 cm)
C.108-1914

22

Decanter and stopper, about 1770.
Decorated in the London workshops of James Giles
Opaque white lead glass, cut on the wheel and gilt
In a sale of Giles' stock at Christies from 21 March to 25 March 1774 several decanters described as 'in vases and laurels' were sold and it is probable they were similar to the present example.
Tilley Collection
Ht $11\frac{1}{2}$ in (29.2 cm)
C.17 & a—1978

23
Sweetmeat dish, about 1750
Lead glass, cut on the wheel
Wheel-cut glass was known in
England in the late seventeenth
century, but facet-cut stems, such
as that supporting this dish, were
not popular before the second
quarter of the eighteenth century.
Sweetmeat dishes formed part of
the table decoration at the
dessert.
Ht 5⅞ in (14.9 cm)
C.494-1925

24
Teapot, about 1760
Lead glass cut on the wheel
Since this pot probably would not
have withstood the heat of water to
make tea, it must be assumed that
it was intended as a novelty to
display the skill of the glass-
blower and cutter.
Ht 5⅜ in (13.6 cm)
C.49-1929.

23

24

25
Decanter and two glasses,
1810-20
Lead glass cut on the wheel
These glasses, which represent the
highest achievement of
English glass cutters, were
supplied to the Prince of Wales,
later George IV, between 1810
and 1820. A large part of the
service from which they come is
still in the Royal Collection.

Unfortunately no account
survives to indicate the supplier,
but it may have been John
Blades, amongst whose papers
sketches of the glasses are
illustrated.
Ht of decanter: 13½ in (34.3 cm)
C.56 & A—1976 C.57—1976
C.179—1980

26
Ice-cream vase, about 1815
Lead glass cut on the wheel
The cutting of this massive piece
has close affinities with that on
the decanter and glasses illustrated
in plate 25 and may be from the
workshops of John Blades or
Apsley Pellatt.
Ht 14¾ in (37.5 cm)
C.211-1931

5, FAIRLIE PLACE, CLIVE STREET, CALCUTTA.

Bought & Mathews & Jones,

GLASS MERCHANTS, &c. &c.

FROM JOHN BLADES, LONDON,
MANUFACTURER TO HIS BRITANNIC MAJESTY,
TO THE HONORABLE UNITED EAST INDIA COMPANY,
AND BY ROYAL FIRMAUN TO HIS MAJESTY THE SHAH OF PERSIA.

A SUPERB ASSORTMENT OF LUSTRES, WALL AND TABLE SHADES, HOOKAHS, DESSERT SERVICES, TOILET AND USEFUL GLASSWARE, CUT AND PLAIN, OF EVERY DESCRIPTION FROM THE ABOVE ESTABLISHMENT.

Sicca Rupees   Annas

27
Sheet of drawings of glass,
probably from the 1840s
they include early-nineteenth
century glass, such as those in
plate 25 probably by the firm of
John Blades and Francis Jones.

28
Bill head of the firm of Matthews
and Jones, glass importers in
Calcutta, about 1825
It is clear that India was a rich
market for English cut glass.

29
Jug, about 1820
Made at the Falcon Glassworks,
Southwark, of Apsley Pellatt
Cut lead glass with a ceramic
inclusion
Apsley Pellatt introduced the
method of enclosing a ceramic
plaque or model called
'sulphides' in glass from France in
1819. The figure here appears to
represent Geography.
Applewheite Abbot Collection
Ht 7¼ in (18.4 cm)
C.16-1978

29

30
Neptune jug, about 1851
By J. G. Green of London,
possibly using a blank by W. H.,
B. and J. Richardson
Lead glass engraved on the wheel
This jug in the classical taste was
exhibited by J. G. Green at the
Great Exhibition of 1851 in
London.
Museum of Practical Geology
Ht 13¼ in (33.7 cm)
4453-1901

31
Finger bowl, about 1862
By Apsley Pellatt and Co. at the
Falcon Glasshouse, Southwark
Lead glass engraved on the wheel
This finger bowl forms part of a
service of glass made for the
newly married Prince and
Princess of Wales (later Edward
VII and Queen Alexandra) and
exhibited by Apsley Pellatt at the
International Exhibition of 1862.
Royal Scottish Museum
Ht 2⅞ in (7.4 cm)
Circ. 620-1467

32
The 'Elgin' jug, 1878
Engraved by Frederick Kny for
Thomas Webb of Stourbridge
Lead glass engraved on the wheel
The 'Elgin' jug takes its name
from the figures from the frieze
of the Parthenon (the Elgin
Marbles) which run around its
body. The intaglio cutting is in
contrast to John Northwood's jug
of comparable design which was
cut in cameo in 1873. The Kny
example was exhibited at the
Paris International Exhibition of
1878.
Ht 14¼ in (36.3 cm)
C.32 & a—1960

33
Bowl, 1884
Engraved by Frank Scheibner for
Stevens and Williams of Brierley
Hill
Lead glass cut on the wheel
This bowl is an example of the
polished cutting known as 'rock-
crystal' which was introduced
from France in the late 1870s.
The engraving on the bowl in
the Chinese taste was designed by
John Northwood and engraved
by Frank Scheibner. The bowl
was acquired from the
International Health Exhibition
of 1884.
Ht 5 in (12.7 cm)
92-1885

33

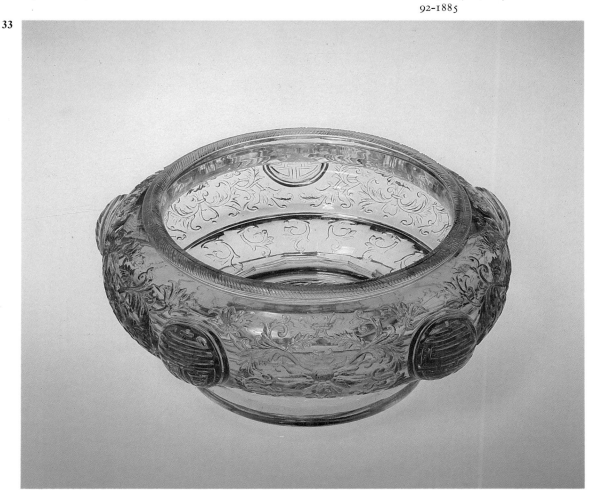

34
Vase, 1884
Engraved by J. T. Fereday on a
blank by Thomas Webb and Sons
Amber glass, cased in opaque
white and cut and engraved
Cameo cut glass gained in
popularity following John
Northwood's production of a
copy of the Portland Vase in
1876. The vase illustrated here
was designed by Thomas
Woodall and executed by J. T.
Fereday, formerly a student at
Dudley School of Art. It was
acquired by the Museum from
the International Health
Exhibition of 1884.
Ht 7⅜ in (18.8 cm)
91-1885

35
Plate, 1837
Made by Thomas Hawkes of
Dudley
Lead glass, cut on the wheel,
probably etched and printed,
painted and gilt
This plate is from a service used
at the first reception given by the
City of London to Queen
Victoria at Guildhall in 1837. The
technique of decoration is far
from clear, apparently combining
cutting, etching, printing, painting
and gilding to achieve a grand
overall effect.
Miss Maud C. Bowes gift
Diam. 8⅞ in (22.6 cm) C.47-1961

36
Roemer, early nineteenth century
Lead glass, cut on the wheel and
decorated with semi-opaque
enamel by John Davenport of
Longport, Staffordshire
Ht 5⅞ in (14.9 cm)
C.49-1966

37
Jug, about 1850
By W. H., B. and J. Richardson
of Wordsley
Opal glass with enamel
decoration, marked on the base
Richardson+Vitrified+Enamel
Colours
The firm of Richardson was
among the leading firms
producing enamelled glass in the
mid-nineteenth century. Others
included George Bacchus in

Birmingham and J. F. Christy in
Lambeth (see plate 38).
R.W. Morris Gift
Ht 9 in (22.8 cm)
C.184-1956

36

38
Water carafe, about 1847
By J. F. Christy of Lambeth
Lead glass painted in enamels and
gilt, signed R. Redgrave ACA
and F.S.
The design for this carafe was
commissioned by Henry Cole in
his alias Felix Summerley from
the artist Richard Redgrave.
Museum of Practical Geology
Ht 10¼ in (26 cm)
4503-1901

39
Goblet, 1876
By James Powell and Sons,
Whitefriars, London
Opalescent glass, mould blown
with trailed decoration
This elegant goblet demonstrates
the work of Powells in the
Venetian taste.
Bought from the manufacturers
Ht 8⅝ in (22 cm)
544-1877

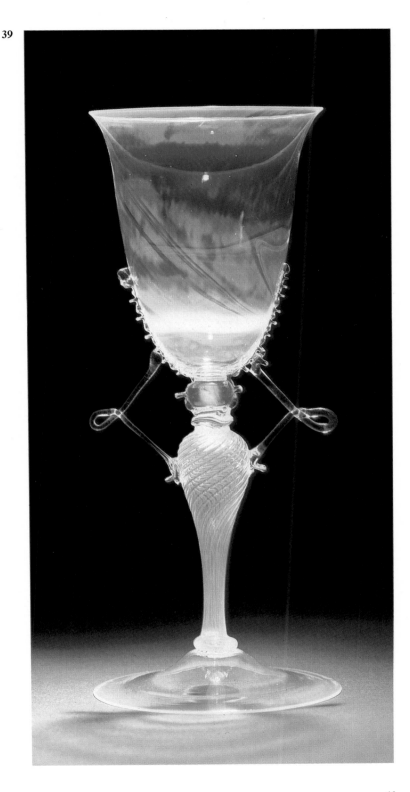

40
Scent bottle, 1831-7
Lead glass, mould blown and cut
on the wheel, by Apsley Pellatt,
at the Falcon Glasshouse,
Southwark
Ht 4¼ in (10.9 cm)
C.83-1982

41
Plate, 1887
Pressed glass, made at Sowerby's
Ellison Glass Works, Gateshead, to
commemorate Queen Victoria's
golden jubilee
Diam 9⅞ in (25 cms)
Circ. 716-1966

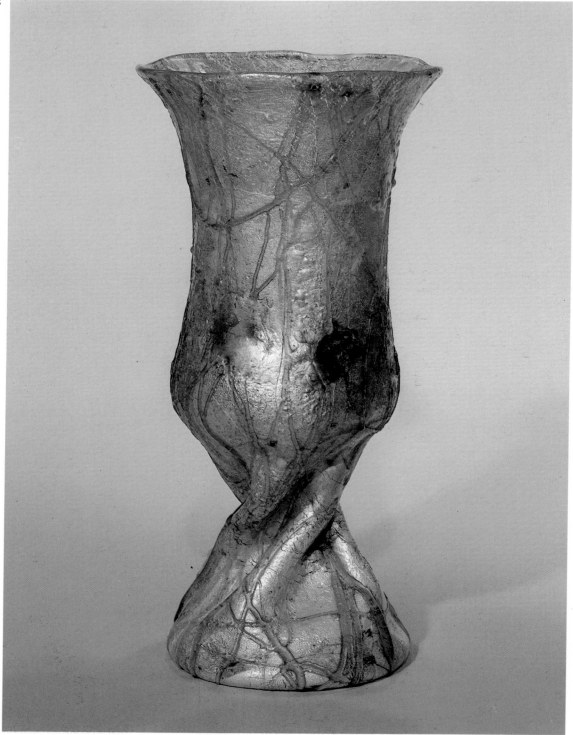

Further Reading

42
Vase, about 1900
Made by Stevens and Williams of
Brierley Hill
Layered glass with silver foil
between, trailed-over in green,
red and yellow
The end of the nineteenth
century saw the vogue for
colourful finishes on glass. This
vase, in a rather organic art-
nouveau style, is of a type known
by Stevens and Williams as
'Silveria'. Other firms produced
similarly striking effects using
different metals and colours.
Ht 12¾ in (32.4 cm)
Circ. 391-1964

No single volume covers the manufacture of English glass to the
same extent as W. A. Thorpe in *A History of English and Irish Glass*
(first published London, 1929, but reprinted in facsimile in 1969).
However, Thorpe, and his contemporary Francis Buckley, whose
History of Old English Glass appeared in 1925, were constricted by
the standards of taste of their day and did not include glass made
after 1830 in their studies. This deficiency has been corrected by
several authors in recent years. Hugh Wakefield's pioneering study
19th Century British Glass was first published in 1961, but a second
edition of 1982 contains new material in the text and illustrations, as
well as a reappraisal of some of his earlier opinions. Barbara Morris's
Victorian Table Glass and Ornaments (London, 1978) is an excellent
survey of the period from 1837. For more specific information on
certain aspects of English glass-making the student would be best
advised to refer to the *Bulletin de l'Association Internationale pour
l'Histoire du Verre*, No. 8 (Liège, 1980) for, despite its title, this
volume contains some of latest information on English glass. There
are articles by Dr Donald Harden ('Pre-Roman Glass' and 'Early
Medieval Glass'), Robert Charleston ('Glass of the High Medieval
Period' and '16th to 17th century English Glass'), Revel Oddy
('British Glass 1680-1830') and Barbara Morris '(British Glass
1830-1900'). Further specialist reading which should be added here is
Eleanor S. Godfrey's excellently researched *The Development of
English Glassmaking 1560-1640* (Oxford 1975), and at the other end
of the temporal spectrum Colin Lattimore's *English 19th Century
Press-moulded Glass* (London, 1979).